Postcards From Twin Peaks

by Benjamin Louche

(as told to Mason Ball)

Copyright © 2017 by Mason Ball

All rights reserved. This book or any portion thereof may not be reproduced or used in any manner whatsoever without the express written permission of the publisher except for the use of brief quotations in a book review.

Printed in the United Kingdom

First Printing, 2017

ISBN 978-1-326-93837-6

www.benjaminlouche.com
www.thedoublerclub.co.uk

Front cover photo: Snoqualmie Falls by Meher Anand Kasam
Licensed under CC BY-SA 3.0
Image modified / cover design by Hard8Studio

"It's a real place. All the characters are real. And the place is real."

- David Lynch

Also by Mason Ball:

Voices In The Red Velvet Elsewhere (2014)

The Menagerie, a fairy tale (with asides) -Illustrated by Jon Attfield- (2015)

Further Voices In The Red Velvet Elsewhere (late 2017)

As Unsong:

A Blue Rose For Black Bob -CD/download- (2014)

All available through The Double R Club

Foreword

Here there be words carved in dream, described in darkness by the flight paths of owls that are not, scorched into red velvet, written backwards, soaked in coffee, wrapped in plastic and floated off on the deepest river of your dreams...

The majority of the poems herein were created for, and performed at, various incarnations of The Double R Club (see *The Club With Two Rs: A Brief History*, page 69), usually by way of introductions to the various performers who had chosen Twin Peaks as inspiration for their act, their moment in the spotlight, their instant in the shadow and strobe.

The poems were spat and spouted at audiences (in various states of excitation and/or bemusement) by myself, that is, a certain part of me, a dreamself and doppelgänger, a projection of a fragment that resides within me; but then, is *he* the projection or am I?

Truth is, this projection/projector, the dreamself (dream-elf?) author of this rhyme and unreason, these curious couplets and odd odes, Mr. Benjamin Louche, would simply not exist were it not for the town of Twin Peaks.

His appearance may lean more in the direction of Lumberton, sinister stomping ground of the felonious and frankly terrifying Frank Booth, but the seed of him was undoubtedly born in that "town where a yellow light still means slow down, not speed up," and indeed in that *other place*, where "the birds sing a pretty song and there's always music in the air."

Witnessing Twin Peaks as it was first broadcast in the UK was a life changing event, taking as it did a regular format that I was familiar with (murder mystery/police procedural) and then turning it most strangely on its ear; but then you will know all of this, no doubt being a fellow convert and enthusiast yourself, you will have had a similar 'Road To Damascus (by way of Sparkwood and 21) Moment', after which nothing was ever quite the same again.

Years later, as if he'd been gestating and festering ever since, Louche sprang to life, my own Lynchian figment, to spout, to recite, to point (sans chemicals) to that which waits for us all in sleep and in somnambulation.

So, Twin Peakers, backwards speakers, loggers, Black Lodgers, Special Agents and one-armed show salesmen, I give you fruit of Louche's heart, words, incantations, questions and secrets to feed your own "dweller on the threshold" and, who knows, perhaps even to give them a good, hard push over the edge.

"Let's rock,"

Mason Ball
(a paltry doppelgänger)

Contents

Postcards From Twin Peaks

You're There Right Now 15
Walking In Fire, Falling In Blood 17
Agent Cooper's On The Case 18
Agent Cooper IS The Case 19
Invocation Of Dark And Troubling Things 20
"Who's the lady with the log?" 21
A Somewhat Irreverent Limerick 22
What Ronette Saw 23
Intercepted Transmission From An Inhabiting Spirit #1 25
Miniature Requiem For A Mynah 26
Diane As Figment 26
We Are Addressed By The Log 28
The Terrible Absence Of Agent Jeffries 29
"This is The Waiting Room..." 31
The Tale of Nadine 32
Coffee As Doorway 34
Corn: Creamed 35
Harold Smith (Misunderstood) 36

A Somewhat Less Than Epic Poem About Pie 38
Josie's End 39
Intercepted Transmission From An Inhabiting Spirit #2 40
"Man... smell those trees..." 41
A Question 42
Poor Laura Palmer 43
Another Question 45
Ballad Of The Blue Rose 46
Mrs. Palmer 47
TBDRAN 48
Intercepted Transmission From An Inhabiting Spirit #3 49
Laura Palmer (In Memoriam) 50
We Are Addressed By The Log A Second Time 51
TMFAP 52
Prayer To A Dark Dream 53
Postcard From Twin Peaks 54

Extras & Asides

Laura Palmer & The Good 'Death' 57
The Great Twin Peaks Coffee Experiment 63
The Club With Two Rs: A Brief History 69

Postcards From Twin Peaks

You're There Right Now

You think you're in a room, you're in a building, in a city,
The air outside a taste of gasoline, architecture not so pretty,
Traffic screams through clouds of discontent, the thrum and push of population,
The noise of engines and machinery, of tintinnabulation.

You THINK that's where you are right now, but you are quite mistaken,
For you are somewhere else, your life a dream from which you will awaken
in ANOTHER PLACE, within these woods, the crack of twig, the scent of pine,
O please don't fight it, you're already here, you have crossed the tree-line.

You are beneath the mighty Douglas firs, within sight of sycamores,
Deep in the belly of Ghostwood, lost in the not-so-great outdoors,
How did you get here? Well, the distance from there to here it ain't so far,
As far as coffee to a piece of pie, from highschool to that old traincar.

And you've arrived on a most portentous day, for things are coming home,

After 25 years "the evil in these woods" is set once more to roam.
What darkness waits between these trees? Why, The Log Lady only knows,
When a young girl screams and the owls do fly, and a lonesome foghorn blows...

Walking In Fire, Falling In Blood

There once was a town called Twin Peaks,
Where girls were pecked with mynah bird beaks,
In the woods, it was said,
Lay a room swathed in red,
From which all evil and horror still leaks.

A young girl called Laura was trapped,
And her soul, it was slowly kidnapped,
Then BOB took her entire,
And she walked into FIRE,
And in plastic forever was wrapped.

Agent Cooper's On The Case

She's dead, she's wrapped in plastic,
Certain things are set in motion,
A small town cries out in grieving,
No one has the faintest notion

just who has done this awful thing,
Just what's been hiding in their midst,
Just how their sleepy little vill
could with such evil coexist.

BUT Agent Cooper's on the case!
And fuelled with coffee black as night
is sure to find the culprit out,
Is sure to fight for what is right!

UNLESS the labyrinth goes deeper,
Than even *he* can comprehend,
And other worlds begin to percolate,
Halt his cause to apprehend

the villain of the piece,
The piece that's left him feeling all a-stupor,
So will this be another triumph
for the dashing Agent Cooper?

Agent Cooper IS The Case

So many years have passed,
Since she was dead and wrapped in plastic,
Since the prom queen fell, a victim,
Reality proven... elastic.

And since the dashing Agent Cooper
entered through those crimson drapes,
And since something it then came out again,
From the place no one escapes,

No, no one escapes that place beyond the fire,
And yet out Cooper came,
That is, something that was quite Cooper-shaped,
But *was* he quite the same?

Truth is, once he had brushed his teeth,
Even he could not be sure,
Could not be sure if he could trust himself,
If his soul remained quite pure,

Or whether something else in fact emerged,
And to this day pretends, because,
Dark things they fly behind his eyes;
Is he who he always was?

Invocation Of Dark And Troubling Things

We conjure now that which happened here,
In the old train car, when the thin veneer
of this world, it wore through, to that OTHER PLACE,
Where darkness walks twixt red velvet, reaches out to embrace
all our fear and our pain, for to feed its desires,
And to send us screaming in shadow, or walking in fires.

For here a man split in twain, he did murder poor Laura,
The homecoming queen, catalyst, the Pandora's
box that loosed secrets the town had turned a blind eye to,
And BOB crept through the curtains, played nightmare peekaboo
and then gorging himself while he revelled in screams,
He left ripples in the deepest river of all our dreams.

For here is BOB's playground, here is his playpen,
Where he relives that which was and which shall be again...

"Who's the lady with the log?"

The Log Lady is the matriarch of the mysteries of Twin Peaks,
Striding strangely through its tragedy and the horrors that it wreaks,
Dismissed as an eccentric, is she insane, or simply cunning?
Her answer to that question? "Wait for tea! The fish aren't running!"

The log itself says nothing, is inscrutable, unspeaking,
Did it truly have the wisdom, have the answers we were seeking?
Did *the log* kill Laura Palmer? Was *it* the font of all this fright?
Was it Killer LOG not Killer BOB? Or is its bark worse than its bite?

Is The Log Lady filled with secrets, is she not so law-abiding?
Does she know more than she's letting on? Just what can she be hiding?
If her layers now were peeled away, whatever would we see?
Would we glimpse terror? Fire? Murders? Or a poem as lovely as a tree...?

A Somewhat Irreverent Limerick

There once was a girl known as Laura,
Who Twin Peaks just missed more-a and more-a,
They wished BOB'd not been so drastic,
As to wrap her in plastic,
But had found a better way for to store-'er.

What Ronette Saw

"I know an old woman who swallowed a fly,"
Well, so says the poem, a fanciful lie,
Yes, but IS IT? Or could a certain truth therein be,
An analogue of dark secrets, dreadful mystery?

I once knew a man who swallowed much more,
Whose throat opened up for a THING to explore,
Whose body, as a boy, became host to shadow,
A man drowning in his life and a man swept below,

A man host to BOB, an inhabiting entity,
Devouring his self, decimating identity,
Pushing poor Leland to unspeakable things,
To bloody deeds, bloodied hands, to internal scorchings.

I once knew a girl who swallowed a darkness,
Who fell away from the light, fell all sunless and helpless,
Fell in tandem with Laura, towards Laura's own end,
And her mind cracked wide open, some ruptures never mend,

For Ronette witnessed secrets, witnessed BOB, witnessed slaughter,
Saw an angel, and flame, a fractured man kill his daughter,
And she ran, and she FLED from her role as voyeur,
Yet those flames would forever after wander with her...

SO, when you open your mouth to scream out, or let in,
Best make sure which it is, lest you predetermine
that your world will combust into endless pyre,
And your dreams will run headless in fear and in FIRE.

Intercepted Transmission From An Inhabiting Spirit
#1

CAN YOU HEAR ME,

              LITTLE CHILD?

THOU BIRD-BONED FRAME,

                        THOU UNDEFILED,

THOU INNOCENCE TASTES GOOD TO EAT,

YOUR TEARS,

                        YOUR CRIES,

ARE THIS MAN'S MEAT.

          I AM NO DREAM,
          THE REAL MCCOY,

     WOULD YOU LIKE TO PLAY WITH FIRE,

                      LITTLE BOY?

Miniature Requiem For A Mynah

We all mourned the passing of Waldo, as his life grew dark and then dimmed,
But who spares a thought for the donuts that his dripping blood ruined?

Diane As Figment

Special Agent Dale Cooper of the FBI,
Sending his voice across the country as the barn owl flies,
Sending tapes, perhaps love letters?
Instruction and flattery,
To a voiceless, faceless woman, to an unknown entity.

A relationship, long distance, professional or intimate?
O so very, very close and yet not nearly proximate,
O this Diane, she is enigma,
She is the wheel within the wheel,
She is the hub of all detection, critical, BUT IS SHE REAL?

But then are YOU real? Or am I? And who can ever truly tell
just who is whose imaginary friend, and who is whose imagined HELL?
And just whatever does it matter?
Just whatever do you care
if his tapes sent across the country are delusion or fervent prayer?

We Are Addressed By The Log

I am a thing inanimate,
Yet animate within,
Within the grip of wood I lie,
Rough bark my only skin.

Was I once a man?
So long of beard and strong of hand?
A cutter among the silent trees,
A heartbeat among the woodland?

A wife perhaps had I,
Yet upon our wedding night,
Perhaps was taken whilst a fire
did roar its wicked, hungry blight.

All through the woods it swept,
Awakened things that upped and stole me,
Stole me from this world of men,
And cast me from reality.

And there I fell in sap,
Fell in knot and fell in grain,
A man locked inside a wooden heart,
Never to breathe again.

And thus I stay, and thus I am,
Within this timber a stifled scream.
Off cut from life I wait and watch,
Driftwood on a town's troubled dream.

The Terrible Absence Of Agent Jeffries

I'm going to leave Judy out of it, but O do tell me true,
Who are you to Philip Jeffries, and who is he to you?
When he vanished all those years ago, screaming at his own downfall,
Leaving behind a scorch mark on a Buenos Aires hotel wall,

Did he manifest in your memory? Did he trouble your slumber?
Did he appear as just one man, or did his doppelgängers outnumber
any presumption of how faces that a normal man can wear?
Did they jump up on the stage, sing songs of darkness and despair?

Have I suffered some bumps on the noggin? Is this not the man
who paraded across the stage, well hung and with a snow white tan?
Major Tom, the Thin White Duke, masks falling in the great elsewhere,
Appearing magically in Philadelphia, "who do you think this is there?"

I've watched that man behind the mask, open mouthed, singing along,
A falling black star, Ziggy played guitar, he played his parts and now he's gone.

He's gone! He's gone! Albert! Albert, call the front desk!
For fates can be kind, they can be cruel, they can be most grotesque,
But Agent Jeffries has left the building, taking his doppelgängers too, I fear,
In fact, I've got the front desk now, and he was never here...

"This is The Waiting Room..."

Twenty five years is a long time to wait,
To wait swathed in red velvet, to ruminate, to collate
all that's happened, occurred, since the moment you died,
Since the angel appeared in darkness, all your futures
denied.

Twenty five winters since the winter that took you,
That snatched you out of this life and hurled you on into
what? Where are you now, and just what have you been
doing
all these years as the world span, your absence imbuing

everything with a shadow, a loss, a Laura-shaped hole
cut into the fabric of all, of a lost, lonely soul.
Tell me where are you now? If indeed anywhere,
A flicker in peripheral vision, a whisper on the stair?

Are you still waiting in the red room, and if waiting, for
what?
Or for *whom* have you been waiting? In evening dress
and coffee pot
beside you; is it Cooper you await? Is it? Because,
I have to warn you, do take heed, he may not be the man
he was...

The Tale of Nadine

A monocular woman named Nadine,
With a temperament far from serene,
Was mad spouse to 'Big Ed',
Who oft' wished he were dead,
For her voice cut like a guillotine...

Her curtains, she said, were too noisy,
Could be heard from Twin Peaks down to Boise,
So she tried and she tried,
That noisiness to hide,
So she'd come off all 'Helen of Troy-sy'.

She went MAD, she went crawling the walls,
She had trips, she had stumbles, had falls,
But of course, what a berk!
She then knew what would work,
The answer, of course: COTTON BALLS!

Yes, our tale it concerns Nadine Hurley,
Who, depressed, thought to leave the world early,
She downed pill after pill,
Hoping herself to kill,
Which then caused a great big Hurley-burly.

But, undying, she fell into coma,
An unconscious somnambulant roamer,
And then woke, a teenager,
(Amnesia, I'd wager)
Went in search of her high school diploma.

And as an ebullient cheerleader in school,
She displayed immense strength, risked misrule,
For she joined the wrestling team,
And proceeded to ream,
All the boys, thus prompting ridicule.

Such delusion could mean chaos, rigmarole,
Such shenanigans take a terrible toll,
A one-eyed woman, quite mad,
With the strength of a tiger? Egad!
A woman quite OUT OF CONTROL!

Coffee As Doorway

That beverage that beckons you into its darkness,
A steaming black portal reaching below the surface
of things that we think of as all that is real,
While other things wait and hunger, their intent to steal
away all that you value, all indeed that you love,
To slide beneath your skin like a hand fits a glove.

Yes, all that exists in your mug as you sup
in that beautiful bitterness contained in your cup,
As the caffeine floods in, who's to say that you're not
being flooded with BOB and just who could say what
else may leak from that other place and into your soul,
For to BE you or KILL you, its ultimate goal.

OR perhaps it's a drink, nothing more, nothing less,
No hidden demons, nor killer, nothing to confess,
Just a cup with the sting of the 48 hour blend,
Your heart to kick start, your hangover to mend,
No backwards speaking, no zigzags, no screaming, no fright,
Just COFFEE: black as midnight on a moonless night.

Corn: Creamed

Creamed corn, creamed corn,
Held in small magician's hands,
From your goo what shall be born?
What will be loosed upon these lands?

Creamed corn in that other place,
Mystery dodging full disclosure,
One girl's death, one town's disgrace,
Her pain and suffering: G A R M O N B O Z I A .

Harold Smith (Misunderstood)

A suicide note scrawled on paper: *J'ai une âme solitaire*, translated as "I am a lonely soul,"
But that's actually not what that means, that's if you even care, not to encourage needless pedantry or undue rigmarole.

J'ai une means "I have a" whereas *Je suis* it means "I am," I'm afraid that the translation is bad,
Though you may roll your eyes and tut, not really give a good goddamn, what if he wasn't saying he *was* one but only claiming that he *had*

one, well, another question arises, if you *had* a lonely soul, like some talisman of hopelessness or trinket of despair,
Would you keep it in the cupboard? Flush it down the toilet bowl? Would you keep it in the hothouse would you braid it in your hair?

But if he *had* a lonely soul, rather than just claiming to be one, just what was this 'soul' of which this poor man spake,
Could it be a certain riddle had been secretively spun, and it's unsolving stand as Cooper's greatest terrible mistake?

What if the 'lonely soul' that Harold had was a riddle that remained unbroken, a mystery that avoided all enquiry,

What if that riddle pointed to all things left unspoken,
what if the 'lonely soul' in fact was Laura Palmer's secret diary?

For what was that diary but a place to keep her inner pain, a repository for a girl out of control,
As she scribbled down her agonies, in between snorts of cocaine,
Well, what was she, in those pages, but a lost and lonely soul?

A Somewhat Less Than Epic Poem About Pie

I think that I shall never spy,
A poem lovely as a pie.

Josie's End

In a drawer pull, something trapped,
Something held forevermore,
Held in nightstand, held in bedroom,
Held behind a hotel door.

Trapped and screaming, though unheard,
The face of Josie in the wood,
In the grain twisted, contorted,
But one thing should be understood.

One question should be asked,
Why, in that hotel alone,
How many drawer pulls might there be?
Can an answer ever be known?

And then go onward with your question,
Push it out beyond opinions,
How many drawer pulls exist in the whole wide world?
Maybe thousands, maybe MILLIONS.

Intercepted Transmission From An Inhabiting Spirit #2

I HEAR EVERYTHING YOU DO,

                                                   GIRL,

      AND TASTE JUST WHAT YOU'RE THINKING.

MY FIRE GROWS WITHIN ME,

      EVEN AS YOUR FLAME IS SHRINKING.

I WILL B E YOU OR I WILL K I L L YOU,

          (AND I'M CLOSER THAN YOU KNOW)

I CAN TURN YOU INSIDE OUT,

                                                   GIRL,

                I CAN PUT ON QUITE SHOW.

I'LL KILL ALL YOU EVER LOVED, GIRL, I WILL

    GO   ON   QUITE   A   SPREE,

AND I ALWAYS SIGN MY WORK, GIRL, YOU SPELL IT:

                                                       B-O-B.

"Man... smell those trees..."

The trees are the tress are the tress are the trees,
But do they sway you soporifically, do they put your mind at ease?

Do they stand as mute witnesses to crimes hiding in the dark?
Do they yearn for conflagration, for that catalystic spark?

What have they seen throughout the years, O just what slaughter, just what hell?
If bark could speak, if leaves converse, the terrible tales that they would tell...

A Question

When the Log Lady told Cooper to "Ask it," and then when he did not,
Was it this moment alone that span us on to two seasons' convoluted plot?
For she stood there and told him to "Ask it," and he simply looked at her askew,
If he *had* asked it and it had told him, would the whole thing have ended in episode two?

Poor Laura Palmer
(sung to the tune of Eleanor Rigby)

Ah, look at all the garmonbozia!
Ah, look at all the garmonbozia!

Poor Laura Palmer, waits wrapped in plastic,
So drastically murdered by persons unknown,
(Cue ominous drone)
Found by Pete Martell, whose fishing trip
had soon tipped into something that speaks of nightmares,
Caught him unawares.

All the garmonbozia,
In clouds of cheap cocaine,
All the garmonbozia,
This suffering and pain.

Agent Dale Cooper, arrives with his Dictaphone
all alone trying to find the one who,
Killed the girl and withdrew,
Look at him hunting calling names in a copse
throwing rocks, sort of Russian roulette,
He talks of Tibet.

All the garmonbozia,
To solve he must transcend,
All the garmonbozia,
Who's your doppelgänger friend?

Ah, look at all the garmonbozia!
Ah, look at all the garmonbozia!

Skulking in shadow, a figure in denim 'n' dreams
with a death-bag 'n' long dirty hair,
Gives us a scare,
He's Killer BOB, well... well if you ask me then honestly
I'd have to say:
Bit of a giveaway.

All the garmonbozia,
The clue is in the name,
All the garmonbozia,
Killer BOB's clearly to blame.

Ah, look at all the garmonbozia!
Ah, look at all the garmonbozia!

Another Question

Josie (swallowed) cries out in vain,
A fate never explained or understood.
But can The Log hear Josie's torment,
Through the medium of wood?

Ballad Of The Blue Rose

What makes a rose blue, and what meaning therein?
Grown behind picket fence or worn on a pin,
Can a rose feel sorrow, can its petals fall like tears?
Can the colour blue hold significance? Can its thorns prick out your fears?

Can they prick your thumbs in warning, that something wicked comes?
Something quite against all nature, something impossible that numbs
all your ability to differentiate between the waking world and dreams?
A thing that doesn't belong, yet ever closer than it seems.

For meaning lies in everything, in blinking eyes, in sour face,
In the thread they used to alter the dress, in Lil walking in place,
But what secrets use the bluest rose for their habitat?
What secrets? Oh, I'm sorry child, but I can't tell you that.

But if you listen oh so carefully, when the nightsea wind doth blow,
You may hear the blue rose singing, and if you do then you will know...

Mrs. Palmer

Mrs. Palmer, Mrs. Palmer, I don't want to alarm ya,
But something's after your Laura and it's aimin' to harm her,

This THING has been hiding, hiding inside your marriage,
Hiding secrets, hiding horrors, planning hurt, planning damage,

It says that if it cannot BE her, why then it will KILL her,
This creature, this spirit, this creamed corn connoisseur,

Mrs. Palmer, you'll scream, the pale horse will arrive,
And the town will run headless and all evil will thrive,

And your daughter will FALL and in darkness be bled,
And will walk there in fire, twixt the zigzags and red.

TBDRAN

The black dog runs at night, the black dog runs at night,
Its owner is a silhouette, his eyes are not quite right.

The dog itself cannot exist, yet it is clearly there,
Its bite is worse than any bark, a red room is its lair.

All innocence is eaten up, all fear and pain devoured,
Girl after girl is murdered there, is ended and deflowered.

In dreams the owls are hunting YOU, *YOUR* name you hear them sing,
You've gone too far to turn back now,

B U T D O N O T T A K E T H E R I N G . . .

***Intercepted Transmission From An Inhabiting Spirit
#3***

THE FATHER PROVED THE PERFECT PATSY,

    AS A VEHICLE:

            ADVANTAGEOUS.

BUT TO PULL THE RIPCORD I WAS FORCED,

    THAT COOPER'S MEDDLING QUITE

           O U T R A G E O U S .

BUT FEAR NOT,

    HE WILL BE PAID IN FULL,

        FOR HIS GROSS INTERFERENCE.

FOR WHILE IT'S TRUE I VANISHED

        INTO

            THIN

                AIR,

HE WILL REGRET MY REAPPEARANCE.

Laura Palmer (In Memoriam)

Ashes to ashes, dust to dust,
Farewell to the drug abuse, farewell to the lust
of a girl who was spiralling, who was falling in flame,
Who was haunted and hunted in a nightmarish game
where her father was BOB and BOB made him *do things*,
Made him violate, murder, by pulling the strings
and by forcing him into INCESTICIDE,
And all the while KILLER BOB used his body to hide.

The air stank of burnt oil and it stank of FOUL PLAY,
And the angels didn't help, because they'd all gone away...

We Are Addressed By The Log A Second Time

I saw something that night,
That night the owls were flying.
And one day I shall tell you all,
And when I do, I won't be lying.

It was dark and there was laughing,
And O so many things were blocked.
Flashlights in the trees, two men, two girls,
While behind another stalked.

The dark was pressing in on her,
The owls were near, unbearable,
Screaming, far away, quiet then,
One man, one voice, so terrible.

And after that, all was silent, was mystery,
And people wept, did ask questions, enquire.
Thinking this a workaday tragedy,
But there can be no smoke without fire.

And as I lay in Margaret's arms,
She the only soul that hears my call,
Curled in my log like a termite,
Mute and blind and yet I SEE ALL.

TMFAP

There is a little man who MOVES
to the music of the spheres,
Epileptic and spasmodic,
To the rhythm of your fears.

As he does the hot-shoe-shuffle
over zigzags, through the screams,
You will feel your body start to move,
Your blood tear at the seams.

You will twitch and you will shimmy,
You will shake to your damnation,
As he speaks in backwards tongues,
This little man, this amputation.

He is known as The Man From Another Place,
To others, simply *HIM*,
The dreaming dancer, the dwarf, the arm,
Some call him THE PHANTOM LIMB.

Prayer To A Dark Dream

Now I lay me down to scream,
Perchance to sleep, perchance to dream,
To swim, to sink, to drown in fire,
To fall in black and dreamy mire…

Now I lay me down to die,
To dream of giants, to dream of pie,
To go too far, to cross that line,
To die a death that is "damn fine."

Postcard From Twin Peaks

We're having a wonderful time,
(Homecoming Queen corpses notwithstanding)
We're going for long woodland walks,
The locals all fine and glad-handing.

We've stuffed ourselves on coffee and donuts,
Climbed the binary mountain range.
Saw a boy magician do tricks with creamed corn,
The woods are wondrous here... but they're strange.

We've a wonderful room at The Great Northern,
Though slept fitfully, our dreams filled with fear,
If you could ignore all the oddness, you'd love it,
The weather is FIRE and we wish you were here...

Extras & Asides

Laura Palmer & The Good 'Death'

I'm not sure I'm going to be able to explain this, but here goes.

I can't tell you how many time I've seen *Fire Walk With Me*. From the time it first came out at the cinema, through the times I've watched it on video, then DVD, then again on the big screen as part of the Twin Peaks UK Festival, and finally on Blu-ray (replete with those delicious *Missing Pieces*); but no matter what the format or venue, that final scene, without fail, always gets me.

I always go cold and I always tear up.

There is something about that final scene that I think describes (maybe 'describes' is not the right word, perhaps 'illustrates'?), that illustrates death better than anything I've ever seen.

But let's get a few things out of the way:

#1 – *Spoilers* of course

#2 – This is not My Grand Theory™ as to what this or that means, this is not an attempt to decode or explain anything. I almost never read fan theories, particularly of Lynch's work, as I find the very idea of them somewhat self-defeating and reductive. This is nothing more than a description of what that scene in particular makes me feel and think.

"It makes me uncomfortable to talk about meanings and things. It's better not to know so much about what things mean. Because the meaning, it's a very personal thing

and the meaning for me is different than the meaning for somebody else."

– David Lynch

#3 – When I say in the title 'Good Death', I refer not to the way in which Laura dies (which is about as far from any definition of 'good' as you could imagine) but to her appearance and *experience* after death. I deliberately chose not to use the term 'afterlife' as personally I do not believe in such a thing and nor do I believe that such a belief (or even suspension of disbelief) is necessary to 'get' *Fire Walk With Me*. Which is all a roundabout way of saying that, in this context, I mean that the way in which she dies is violent and dreadful, but her 'death' is what follows that: her state of being dead.

But let me describe the scene. Following her brutal murder and BOB / Leland's return to The Black Lodge / Red Room, the close up of the monkey and the slow motion discovery of her body (anyone who hasn't seen the film now likely thinks I've had some kind of stroke), the camera moves slowly across the brown and cream chevron floor (no, it *isn't* black and white! Don't get me started) towards the red curtains; then we see Laura, seated. Standing beside her, his hand on her shoulder, is Agent Cooper. She's looking up at him, perhaps sadly, perhaps hopefully; he is smiling down at her. A realisation seems to hit her (perhaps of her death?) and she looks away. There is a flash of light and we see an angel. Laura begins to cry, but also to smile, then to laugh, all the time tears rolling down her cheeks. The camera pulls back and credits roll over a still of her face, framed in blinding light, smiling.

Gets me every time.

For me this illustrates death in such an incredibly original and moving way. We've seen the terrible things that have happened to Laura, we've followed her throughout her last seven days, and indeed watched the aftermath of her murder before even that. Her reaction to her own death feels so natural and unexpected, her tears, tears of relief, of joy, at the realisation that her suffering and pain is over; her laughter perhaps also of relief, but also at the horrific absurdity of life. Add to that Sheryl Lee's frankly impossibly emotionally intricate and convincing performance throughout the film and I'm knocked sideways at every single viewing. It's not of course a happy ending, but it remains, to me at least, a strangely uplifting one.

"At the centre of it an absolutely fantastic performance by Sheryl Lee, a performance of operatic intensity. Frankly, I don't care who else was nominated for Oscars that year, the fact that she was overlooked because no one liked the movie that she was in, is shameful."

— Mark Kermode

So, Lynch fan likes Lynch film, so what, right? Well fair point but that scene also had a strange resonance for me in a place I absolutely didn't expect it to appear. Let me explain.

October 2014; I was lucky enough to be appearing in Dickie Beau's strange and moving production *Camera*

Lucida at The Barbican. As part of the rehearsal process we all went along to a 're-birthing' workshop.

Re-birthing, as I understand it, is a way to A) deal with trauma supposedly created at your birth and B) sometimes to regress you to a former life. Now, full disclosure, I find the first of these ideas somewhat dubious and the second I don't believe in *at all*. But I thought, in for a penny, we're doing this as a cast, so let's see what happens.

We were told to lie on the floor, the room was darkened. We were then taught a particular rhythmic breathing method which we all then adhered to for the next hour. We closed our eyes.

Over the next hour several strange things happened.

Some experienced odd sensations, others said they felt the pain from physical injuries long since healed, I think one of us fell asleep (no, it wasn't me). My arms, which started relaxed by my sides, over time contracted, bringing my hands into claws beside my face, which also contorted strangely (more strangely than usual). When the exercise was over, a number of us, myself included, spoke of 'seeing things' during the process.

Now. It seems very logical indeed to me that if you breathe in a certain way whilst lying down in a dark room, that the oxygen flow to your brain will be altered and thus so will your mental state. Nothing problematic there. There could also be something along the lines of self-hypnosis going on, a kind of trance state; again, no problem. So when I say that I saw things, I speak of something approaching a kind of conscious dreaming.

I saw, and will tell you, THREE things.

#1 – The first was my wife's face, smiling, she does that rather well.

#2 – The second was the outline of a body, I think male, falling in space, against a starfield.

#3 – The third was Laura Palmer's face from the final scene of *Fire Walk With Me*, laughing and crying.

    Afterwards, describing these things to the others I was struck by just how deeply this scene has been implanted in my subconscious (together with just how contrary my mind has to be to make a 'birthing' exercise all about death and the inherent ridiculousness of it).

~

POSTSCRIPTUM, from *The Missing Pieces*:

Doc Hayward: "The angels will return. And when you see the one that's meant to help you, you will weep with joy."

The Great Twin Peaks Coffee Experiment

Now, all who know of David Lynch and his work, in particular Twin Peaks, will know of his interest, nay *obsession*, with coffee; and all who know me will know that despite my interest nay obsession, with David Lynch, I am not a coffee drinker... and therefore a failure in life.

Or am I? (rhetorical question, let's not pick at *that* thread).

Because, what if, and bear with my wilfully circuitous logic here, what if coffee, far from being an escape into the good life of palpitative euphoria, what if it is in fact the source of all that is bad? *Think about it*. In Twin Peaks they all drink coffee all the time, right? And terrible things happen to them *all the time*; coincidence? (see page 34).

Yet still my coffee-less existence weighs on me. So I have decided to embark on an experiment.

Following a theory passed on by one of The Double R Club's 52 card pick up girls, the lovely Yvonne (the 8 of hearts, freshly scented from the perfume counter at Horne's Department Store) that, should a non coffee drinker drink a cup of coffee every day for eight consecutive days, then he or she would then acquire a taste for said hot beverage. Can this be true? Or must it be mere nonsense? Is the number eight magical somehow, or arbitrary? And if not eight, how many days would it take, if indeed it was possible *at all*? And should I find the taste for it, will terrible, dark and troubling things then begin to happen to me as a result?

At the time of writing it is early 2017, year of season 3, and so it seemed apposite to conduct this experiment of daily coffee intake with a daily re-watch of season 1 of Twin Peaks (no bingeing, one episode per day), and to imbibe only David Lynch 'Signature Cup' Coffee; what follows is the result...

Day #1 - Pilot - "Northwest Passage"
coffee: milk, one sugar (white)

The overpowering bitterness of my previous forays into the world of coffee was pleasantly less powerful that I had feared. The coffee could have been a little hotter but I got distracted by the episode and forgot to drink up quickly. The aftertaste was oddly warming.

- Cooper drinks a coffee from a polystyrene cup in the sheriff's office, the scene leaving me wondering, not for the first time, just who the hell is going to eat all those bloody donuts?

Day #2 - Episode 1 - "Traces to Nowhere"
coffee: milk, one sugar (white)

Hmm. Something of a step backwards. The burnt/bitter flavour felt a little... 'flatter' somehow, less depth; perhaps something to do with our dinner an hour or so previous of Piri Piri chicken?

- Cooper gives the immortal line "This is, excuse me, a damn fine cup of coffee" in the Great Northern Dining Room.

Day #3 - Episode 2 - "Zen, or the Skill to Catch a Killer"
coffee: milk, one sugar (brown)

Not too much to report, no great developments or epiphanies. Not sure the brown sugar made much difference. The whole eight day theory is beginning to feel somewhat spurious. Still, on I go. Maybe the addition of a donut tomorrow...?

- Cooper drinks coffee in the woods prior to the rock-throwing; the bottle breaks on the name *Leo Johnson*.

Day #4 - Episode 3 - "Rest in Pain"
coffee: milk, one sugar (brown),
donut: plain, ring, chocolate frosting

Coffee and donut. But would the clash of the bitter and the sweet only serve to make the bitter bitterer? It would seem not. Something about the "taste sensation" when coffee collides with donut works really rather well. Easily my favourite cup so far; I'm hoping that's not just because I *really* like donuts...

- Cooper learns of the existence of The Bookhouse Boys over coffee and huckleberry pie at The RR.

Day #5 - Episode 4 - "The One-Armed Man"
coffee: milk, one sugar (white)
donut: plain, ring, glazed

I actually rather enjoyed moments of that cup. In between bites of donut. *Was* it just the donut? (Although the donut itself was not as good as last night's.) I was left with the wish that the cup had been larger. Hmmm. Am I falling under coffee's spell? Should I fear my dreams this evening?

- Extra coffee is required to plough through the files from Dr. Lydecker's veterinarian office.

Day #6 - Episode 5 - "Cooper's Dreams"
coffee: milk, one sugar (white)

I have switched from our limited edition RR coffee cup to a larger mug. Donuts, or complimentary foodstuffs of any kind, have been eschewed until I work out just whether they have unduly influenced my reactions these last two nights. Post coffee reaction: Yeah maybe I *do* just really like donuts. Bitter, and while not so much unpleasant, not quite far enough in the other direction either. Hmmm, not a good sign for my ultimate conversion. Also, and I'm genuinely not making this up, last night my wife Rose woke up with the smell of scorched engine oil in her nostrils, so much so that she got up and checked the flat; there was nothing.

- Cooper is in dire need of coffee due to missed sleep because of "a large group of insane men" staying on his floor at The Great Northern.

Day #7 - Episode 6 - "Realization Time"
coffee: milk, two sugars (muscovado)

Back to the smaller cup, and I've chosen to add muscovado sugar, upping the dose to two. So, a sweeter cup certainly, but one no more... moreish than the last. One day to go of the experiment and the chance of coffee winning me over seems slim to none.

- Cooper gives his "Every day, once a day, give yourself a present" speech to Harry. He's talking, of course, about "two cups of hot, black coffee."

Day #8 - Episode 7 - "The Last Evening"
coffee: milk, two sugars (muscovado), cherry pie

Having avoided comestible accompaniment for the last two nights, it seemed only fitting to end the experiment by drinking my last cup of coffee alongside a slice of cherry pie. *Damn* that pie was good.

- It would appear, and correct me if I'm wrong, but is this the only episode in season one in which no coffee is drunk? Is this a sign?

RESULT:

    I fear, even after the full eight days proscribed, I remain a non-coffee drinker. That's not to say that I did not enjoy a few of those cups but, for me at least, coffee works best with food and not as my go-to hot beverage pick-me-up of choice. It seems that I have as British a palate and I do a British pallor.
    So, to reiterate, I remain, ostensibly, a non-coffee drinker.
    Though, looking on the bright side, with regards to my theory about coffee being a 'doorway' to dark and troubling things, I also remain unplagued with backwards-speaking dreams of zig-zagged rooms and, as yet, no gurning, dirty-haired, double-denimed demon or inhabiting spirit has crawled in through my bedroom window; I say again, *as yet...*

The Club With Two Rs: A Brief History

2008: I was hip deep in coursework studying for a degree in creative writing. Though I'd previously studied acting and physical theatre, at that point I hadn't actually been on stage in years. My wife, Rose Thorne, a professional chef when we met, had been treading the boards up and down the country for roughly two years as a burlesque performer.

Having been brought into this world of cabaret and burlesque as 'the other half' of a performer, I was able to view the scene as something of an outsider. And then, just when I had more than enough to think about, what with coursework etc., an idea began to form; in Lynchian parlance, I had hooked a "Big Fish."

The idea was that of a cabaret and burlesque show with a difference. Something stranger, darker, less... immediately comforting for the audience.

Both Rose and I were long time fans of David Lynch, years before we met, and it seemed that perhaps Lynch's work could serve as a perfect framing device for this show idea. Thinking of so much of his work, there seemed to be many examples of some performance space or other within the narrative, and not a million miles away from a cabaret stage: *Twin Peaks* has its Road House, *Blue Velvet* The Slow Club, *Lost Highway* The Luna Lounge, even *Eraserhead* has the stage in the radiator; the idea festered and grew.

Now *I* may have hooked the fish but it sure as hell took both of us to reel it in, to land it, adding touches here and there, defining a format, the tone, just how this thing might work, if indeed work it would.

Problem #1 was: Where to stage this strange animal of a show?

While attending Jo King's now legendary *Tournament Of Tease* burlesque competition, upstairs at Bethnal Green Working Men's Club, we found the answer to our question. Not only did the venue have Peaksian wooden panelling, red wall lighting and red curtains, it also had its trademark Lynchian-as-all-get-out illuminated love heart on the stage. And if that wasn't perfect enough, one of those performing that very night was Emerald Fontaine, who did an act to The Pink Room from *Fire Walk With Me*; and lo, our idea had a home (and our first show had a first act on the bill in Ms. Fontaine!)

But what to call ourselves? As I recall 'The Pink Room' was a consideration (since taken up by the lovely Francine The Lucid Dream and her cohorts in NYC), as were many, very likely poorer ideas; but when Rose hit upon 'The Double R Club' everything fell into place.

(As an interesting side note, it was only after we started that we discovered there had been a club called *The Double R*, also in east London, way back in the sixties; run by the notorious Ronnie and Reggie Kray)

Though all of Lynch's oeuvre was to be our inspiration, it was indeed apposite to choose as our name a reference to *Twin Peaks*, the TV series being far and away his most well known project to date, and in fact the very thing that got both of us interested in his work in the first place. It should be noted however that we have never tried to 'place' the event as happening *at* the Double R Diner, but merely share part of our name with that fine establishment, and as such have never specified just what *our* two Rs might stand for -Rest and Relaxation? Rules and Regulations? Rock and Roll? Red... Rabbit? (we'll never tell).

Our first decision was to make the night not simply a slavish in-joke or an elitist aficionado-only evening. Geeky at times, yes, but never so much so that it excludes anyone who doesn't know a particular reference or character, our tag line is "inspired directly, *or indirectly*, by the dark and beautiful worlds of David Lynch" and so we are. After eight years we've distilled it down into a certain kind of mood, a tone, something just a little 'off', just a hair different; something dark (but never gothic), something strange (but never frivolous), something unnerving, absurd and often unexpected.

We have, I think, carved out and defined our own particular brand of Lynchian oddity, perhaps a little anglicised in places, but which clearly resonates with our regulars -a short survey revealed that many people had literally been given bad (or at the very least strange) dreams as a direct result of The Double R Club.

Since we began in September of 2009 we've staged monthly shows at Bethnal Green (excluding July and August -because even in London it's too damn hot, and December -because we're not exactly festive) and each June we stage our Miss Twin Peaks Contest. We've staged events at London Wonderground, where, given the superior space and technical facilities available our shows become a great deal stranger and a great deal darker; we've also been a big part of every Twin Peaks UK Festival since its inception in 2010, performing for fans and cast members alike.

At the 2015 festival, founder Lindsey Bowen commissioned the building of a replica of the train car in which Laura Palmer was murdered, and The Double R team staged a recreation of that murder a gruelling 11 times over the weekend, replete with mound of earth, 'Fire Walk With Me' note, the scent of damp earth and thunderstorms, and lit only by torch in haze-filled, almost pitch-black darkness. Three of our most loyal performers (Lydia Darling, Snake Fervor and Heavy Metal Pete) went through hell time and again for the unease-inducing entertainment of festival goers and visiting *Twin Peaks* cast members alike (the lovely Sherilyn Fenn hid her face in fear for a great portion of the performance!). To date *The Murder of Laura Palmer* stands as one of our proudest achievements -well that, and the profound physical reaction we garnered from one particular audience member at our 2015 Wonderground show (find us after a show, ask us and we *might* tell you the story...).

My wife and I have undertaken many creative projects in our decades together, in different guises, styles and formats: theatre, club nights, outdoor performances, and to various degrees of success and / or abject failure; though none have been as popular, satisfying, nor multiple award winning, nor could boast the longevity of our own little red velvet elsewhere "filled with secrets," The Double R Club.

If ever you're nearby when it happens again, we'd be glad to welcome you into our dream, with the proviso that we would then walk all over yours...

"Massive, m a s s i v e quantities" of THANKS

To all our Bookhouse Boys & Girls who have, over the years, made The Double R Club (and by extension the work herein) possible:

Rose Thorne (queen of diamonds, queen of the Double R, my wife and organ grinder to my monkey -not the particular euphemism you're picturing), Louise Holland (3 of hearts), Yvonne Holland (8 of hearts), Abbi De Carteret-Feazey (7 of diamonds), Ruth Elizabeth Young (queen of clubs), Sadie Hill (9 of spades), Lain Freefall (2 of spades), Emerald Fontaine (joker), Violet Crumble (jack of clubs), Mina Dutton (6 of spades), Amelie Soleil (queen of spades), Nathan Evans, Sin Bozkurt, Sean 'Magic' Mooney, Amelia Kallman, ReeRee Rockette, Ed Wills, Philip Roast (Hard8Studio), Lindsey Bowden and the Twin Peaks UK Festival, Warren Dent, Charlotte West-Williams, Steve and all at Bethnal Green Working Men's Club.

To the creators of Twin Peaks / Fire Walk With Me: David Lynch, Mark Frost and Robert Engles.

Not to mention all the performers, too numerous to mention, whose acts have inspired so much of this book's content.

I raise an (albeit notional) cup of Joe to you all; I'll see you in the trees...

www.ingramcontent.com/pod-product-compliance
Ingram Content Group UK Ltd.
Pitfield, Milton Keynes, MK11 3LW, UK
UKHW021335271025
8615UKWH00047B/1388